AR PTS: 0.5

D0772218

BRAIN

Shannon Caster

PowerKiDS press

New York

For my grandfathers, Joe and Irie Lee

Published in 2010 by The Rosen Publishing Group, Inc.
29 East 21st Street, New York, NY 10010

First Edition

Editor: Joanne Randolph
Book Design: Greg Tucker
Layout Design: Kate Laczynski
Photo Researcher: Jessica Gerweck

Photo Credits: Cover, pp. 6, 10 (inset), 13, 17, 21 3D4Medical.com/Getty Images; p. 5 Tony Graham/Getty Images; pp. 6 (inset), 14, 18 Shutterstock.com; p. 9 Betsie Van der Meer/Getty Images; pp. 9 (inset), 14 3D Clinic/Getty Images; p. 10 Alistair Berg/Getty Images; p. 13 (inset) © www.istockphoto.com/Bonnie Jacobs; p. 17 (inset) Bambu Productions/Getty Images; p. 18 (inset) Dr. Don Fawcett/Getty Images.

Library of Congress Cataloging-in-Publication Data

Caster, Shannon.
  Brain / Shannon Caster. — 1st ed.
     p. cm. — (Body works)
  Includes index.
  ISBN 978-1-4358-9368-9 (library binding) — ISBN 978-1-4358-9824-0 (pbk.) — ISBN 978-1-4358-9825-7 (6-pack)
  1. Brain—Juvenile literature. I. Title.
  QP361.5.C375 2010
  612.8'2—dc22
                              2009033417

Manufactured in the United States of America

CPSIA Compliance Information: Batch #WW10PK: For Further Information contact Rosen Publishing, New York, New York at 1-800-237-9932

Contents

The Center of It All

Whether you are reading a book, jumping rope, or eating an apple, there is one **organ** in your body that controls all these actions and more. It is your brain! The brain works hard to keep your body running smoothly.

The brain and spinal cord make up the central **nervous system**. Together, these two organs act as the body's command center. They send and receive **signals** from every part of the body. Different parts of the brain are in charge of sending and receiving all these signals. Some of the main parts of the brain are the cerebrum, the cerebellum, and the brain stem.

The cerebrum is the biggest part of the brain. The cerebellum and brain stem are smaller, but they have important jobs to do.

Cerebrum

Brain Stem

Cerebellum

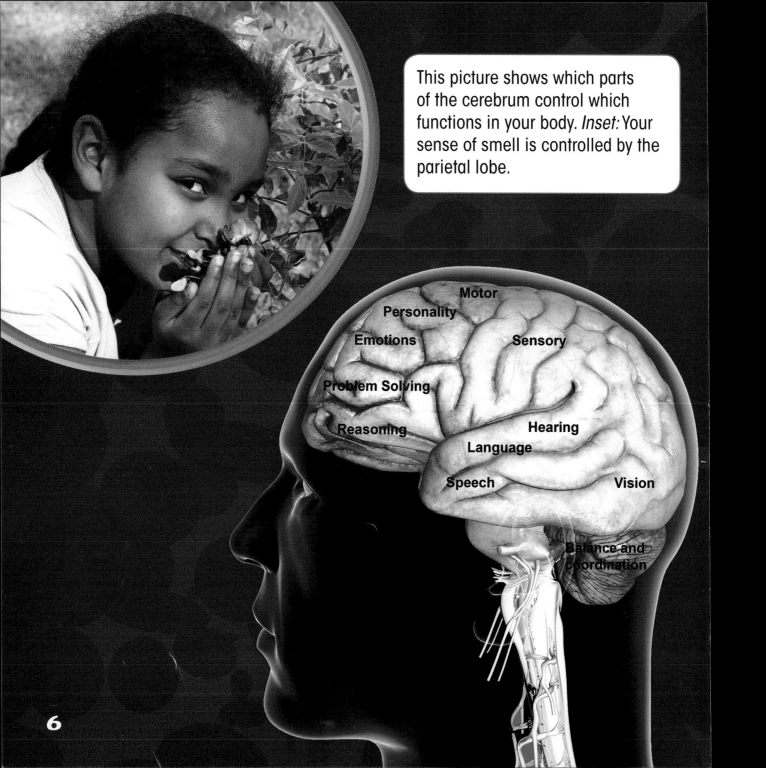

This picture shows which parts of the cerebrum control which functions in your body. *Inset:* Your sense of smell is controlled by the parietal lobe.

Motor

Personality

Emotions

Sensory

Problem Solving

Reasoning

Hearing

Language

Speech

Vision

Balance and coordination

Let's Think About It

Place your hands on top of your head. The part of your brain below your hands is the cerebrum. The cerebrum is the brain's largest part. It makes up 85 percent of your brain's total weight! Scientists often divide the cerebrum into different parts, called lobes. The lobes are the frontal, parietal, occipital, and temporal lobes.

The cerebrum has many functions. It controls your sense of touch, smell, hearing, taste, and sight. It also controls your feelings. When you are happy or angry, this is your cerebrum at work. The cerebrum oversees movement and voluntary actions, or actions you control. The cerebrum is also in charge of thinking and learning.

Two Halves Make a Whole —

Your cerebrum is divided into two halves, or hemispheres. The corpus callosum, a thick band of **nerves**, connects the two sides. These nerves help the sides communicate, or share data, with each other. This communication helps your brain and body act as one.

Each side of your cerebrum is in charge of different things. The left hemisphere controls movements in your body's right side. It also controls skills such as speech and the ability to do math. The right hemisphere controls movements on your body's left side. Skills such as making art and remembering faces come from the brain's right side, too.

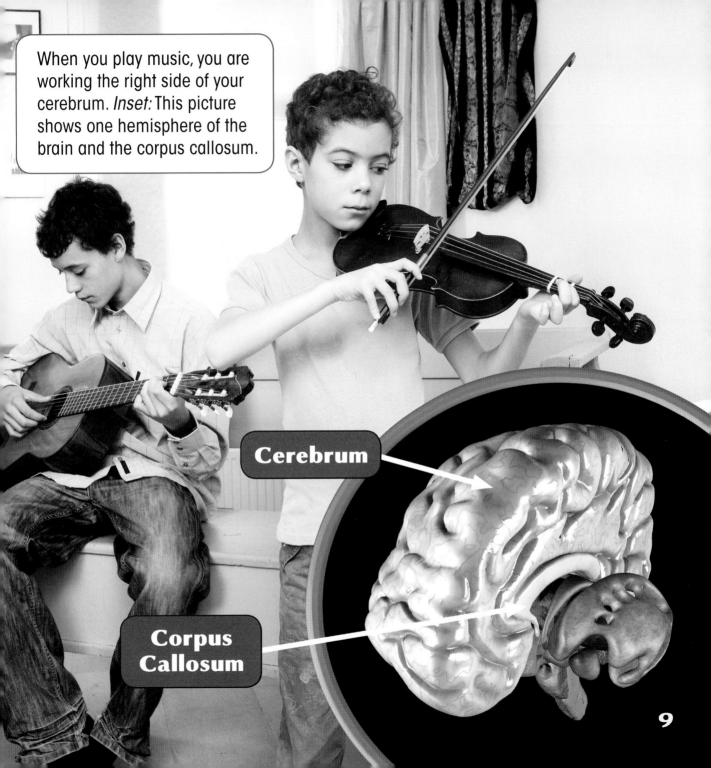

When you play music, you are working the right side of your cerebrum. *Inset:* This picture shows one hemisphere of the brain and the corpus callosum.

Cerebrum

Corpus Callosum

9

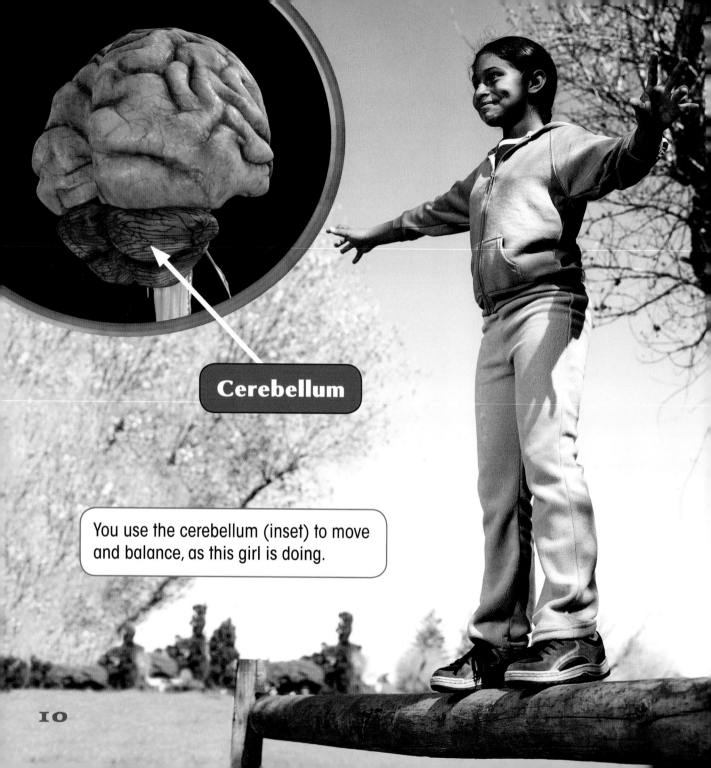

Cerebellum

You use the cerebellum (inset) to move and balance, as this girl is doing.

A Balancing Act

Place one hand on the back of your head just above your neck. Right under your hand is your cerebellum. The cerebellum is often nicknamed the little brain.

Your cerebellum helps **coordinate** muscle movement, balance, and posture. When you climb a ladder, your cerebrum sends messages to your leg muscles. The cerebrum needs the help of the cerebellum, though. Without its fine-tuning, you might fall off the ladder. Your cerebellum helps move your body in a coordinated way, one leg at a time. It also moves smaller muscles and takes in information from your senses to help keep your center of balance.

No Thinking Required

The smallest part of your brain is the brain stem. It is located at the top of your spinal cord. This tiny part of your brain controls many actions in your body that must happen for you to live. The brain stem controls important jobs such as breathing, **digestion**, and your **heart rate**. Because these actions do not require us to think about them, they are called involuntary actions, or actions that happen on their own.

The brain stem also controls some of your **reflexes**. Swallowing, vomiting, and the way your **pupils** dilate, or open up, when a bright light shines in your eyes are all controlled by the brain stem.

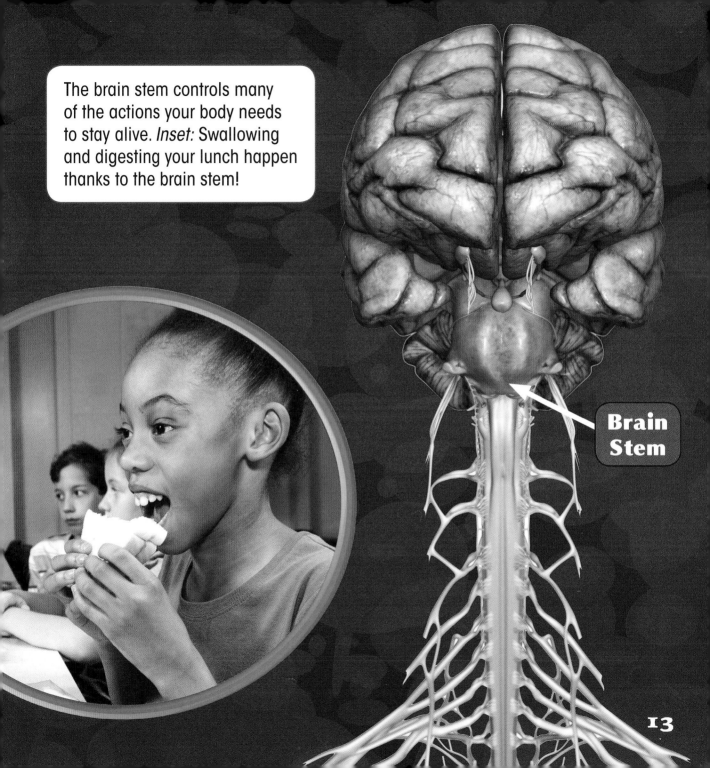

The brain stem controls many of the actions your body needs to stay alive. *Inset:* Swallowing and digesting your lunch happen thanks to the brain stem!

Brain Stem

When we sleep and wake up are controlled by the hypothalamus. *Inset:* The hypothalamus works to keep your body's systems in balance.

Hypothalamus

Body Heat and Sleep

Another part in your brain that has many important jobs is the hypothalamus. It works with other systems in your body to control blood flow, the amount of **nutrients** and salts in your blood, and your body's temperature. When you get too hot or too cold, your hypothalamus helps your body cool off or warm up.

The hypothalamus also helps your body sleep and wake up at the right time. During the day, the hypothalamus helps keep you awake. When night comes, the hypothalamus helps turn off signals that keep you awake. The next time you enjoy a good night's sleep, thank your hypothalamus!

Growing with the Pituitary Gland

At the base of your brain is a small **gland** called the pituitary gland. This lima bean-sized gland controls the release of hormones, which act as **chemical** messengers for the body. The pituitary gland is controlled by the hypothalamus.

One of the hormones the pituitary gland releases is growth hormone. Growth hormone causes your bones and muscles to grow. The pituitary gland also releases hormones that control the amount of melanin produced by your skin. Melanin is the chemical that gives skin its color. The pituitary gland releases hormones that control everything from your kidneys to your thyroid gland.

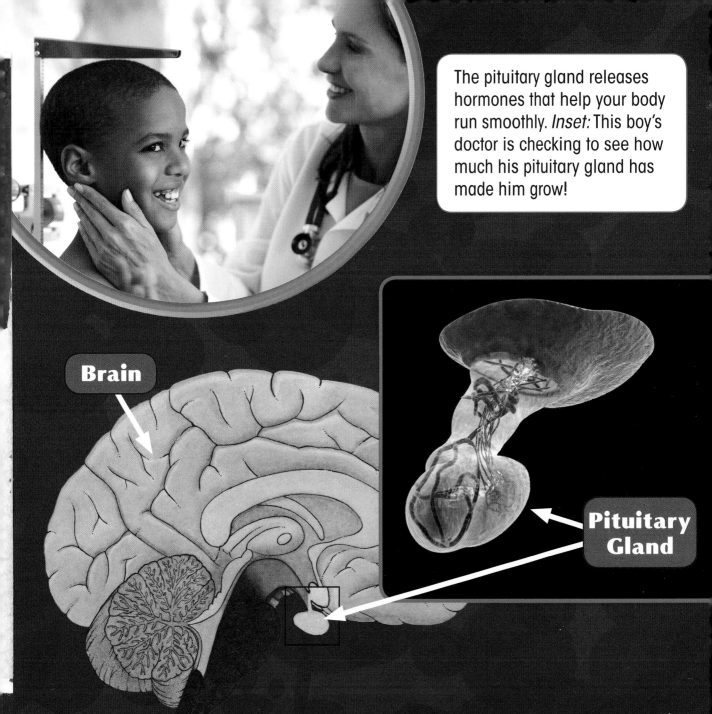

The pituitary gland releases hormones that help your body run smoothly. *Inset:* This boy's doctor is checking to see how much his pituitary gland has made him grow!

Brain

Pituitary Gland

We can run, jump, and play because our brain sends messages along the nerves telling our body what to do. *Inset:* Many synapses connect to this neuron.

Synapses

Neuron

Message Received

   In order for your brain to get messages to and from your body, it uses a system of neurons and synapses. Messages between the brain and body are sent along nerves. The nerves are made up of nerve cells called neurons. When a neuron receives a message, it passes it along to the next neuron in line, kind of like runners in a relay race.

   Between each neuron is a synapse. This synapse includes a small gap that the messages must jump over. Chemicals in your body help the electrical messages jump over the synapses. Faster than you can say "relay race," these messages race along the nervous system!

Remember the Hippocampus—

We use our brain to store new memories and remember old information. How and where those memories are stored is partly controlled by the sea horse-shaped hippocampus.

Let's say we want to remember a set of numbers for a few minutes. Our hippocampus will help store these numbers in our short-term memory. However, when we learn a song, our hippocampus makes sure that information is stored in our long-term auditory memory for us to remember later. The hippocampus directs memories to locations in the brain that will best help us later remember and use the information.

This picture shows where the hippocampus is found in the brain. The other parts shown here help the hippocampus communicate with the rest of the brain.

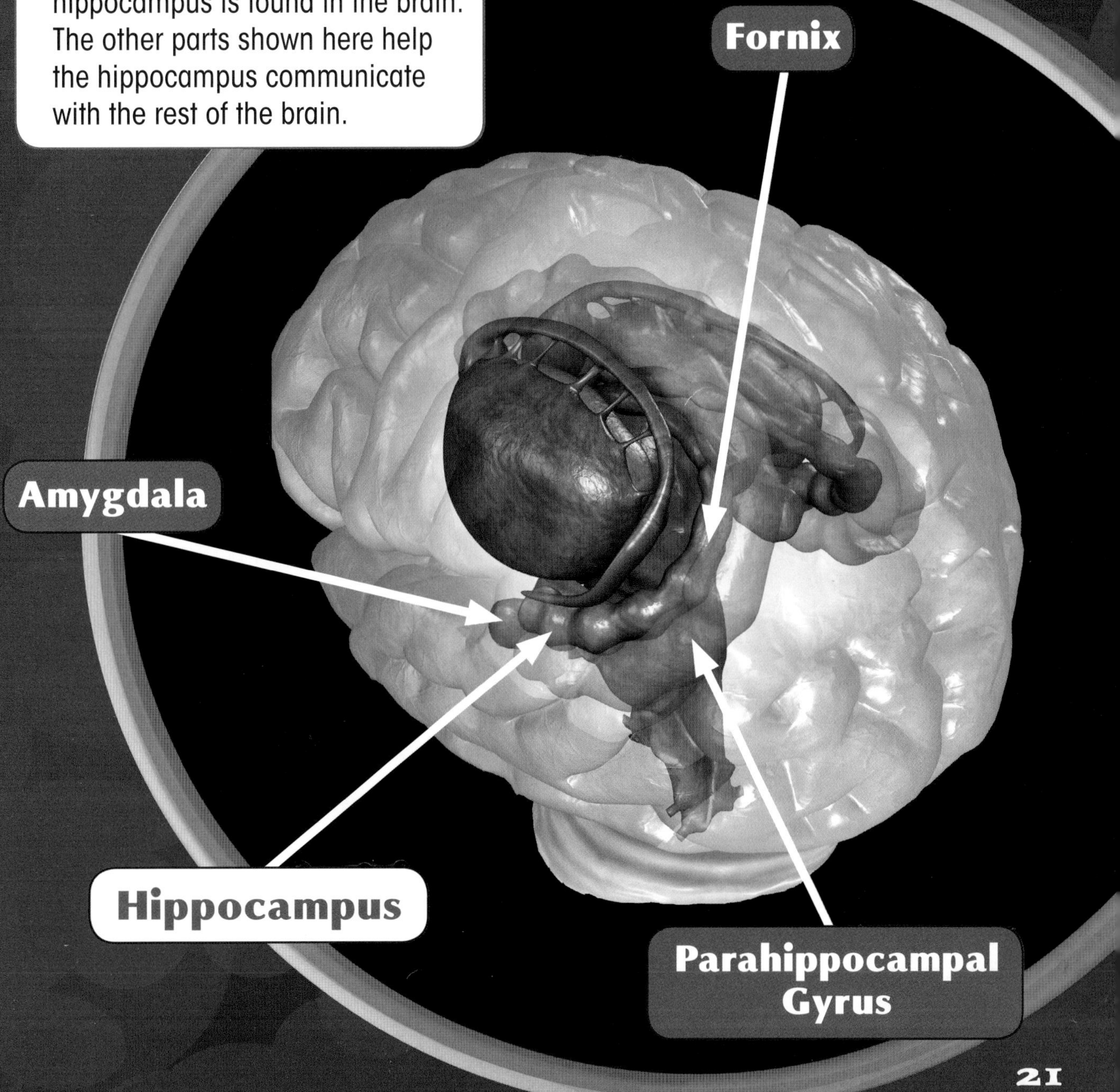

Fornix

Amygdala

Hippocampus

Parahippocampal Gyrus

The Brain in Trouble

Sometimes people's brains may not work as they are supposed to. Alzheimer's disease and cancer are some illnesses of the brain. Most people will never have these problems, though your brain could be hurt in other ways.

Your brain is kept safe from some injuries by the skull, or the bones around your brain. However, a hard hit to the head can still hurt your brain. Be sure to wear a helmet to keep your brain safe when doing activities in which you could hit your head. It is also important to eat healthy foods and get plenty of rest. Your brain takes care of your body, but you need to take care of it, too!

Glossary

chemical (KEH-mih-kul) Matter that can be mixed with other matter to cause changes.

coordinate (koh-OR-din-ayt) To work in a smooth way.

digestion (dy-JEST-shun) Breaking down food so that the body can use it.

gland (GLAND) An organ or a part of the body that produces an element to help with a bodily function.

heart rate (HART RAYT) The number of times your heart beats in one minute.

nerves (NERVZ) Groups of fibers that carry messages between the brain and other parts of the body.

nervous system (NER-vus SIS-tum) Groupings of nerve fibers in people or animals.

nutrients (NOO-tree-unts) Food that a living thing needs to live and grow.

organ (OR-gen) A part inside the body that does a job.

pupils (PYOO-pulz) Openings in the eyes that change size to let the right amount of light into the eye.

reflexes (REE-fleks-ez) Actions that happen without thought.

signals (SIG-nulz) Currents, messages, or sounds that are sent.

Index

Web Sites

Due to the changing nature of Internet links, PowerKids Press has developed an online list of Web sites related to the subject of this book. This site is updated regularly. Please use this link to access the list:
www.powerkidslinks.com/hybw/brain/